All Too Much for Oliver

To the people who matter to me the most, and to the boy who inspired me to do something meaningful

L.B.

To my Mum, my Dad, my two little kids and one big kid

B.M.

First published in 2015 by My Quiet Adventures

www.myquietadventures.com

ISBN: 978-981-09-7755-9

Consultant Editor - Ruth Martin

9 8 7 6 5 4 3 2 1

Printed in the United States of America

The text of this book was set in Print Bold. The artwork was created using pencil and watercolors.

All Too Much for Oliver

Written by Leila Boukarim
Illustrated by Barbara Moxham

This is a story about a little boy named Oliver.

Oliver didn't like being in noisy places. He stayed away from the playground when it was crowded, he thought the music at parties was much too loud, and the zoo was just too much to bear.

In fact, Oliver quite enjoyed playing by himself in his own quiet room.

As they drove back home from the grocery store one day, Oliver and his mom saw some of the neighborhood kids swimming with their parents and playing by the pool. "What do you say we go get our swimsuits on and join them, Oliver?" his mom asked. Oliver gazed out the car window, and even though it looked like fun, Oliver just said, "No thanks, Mom. I just want to play in my room."

The next day, Oliver and his mom went out for a walk in the park near their house. The park was a quiet place, which Oliver liked very much.

It was a beautiful day, and Oliver thought it would be nice to visit the little playground there.

As Oliver and his mom got closer,
the sounds coming from the playground got louder

... and louder

... and louder!

When they finally got there, Oliver changed his mind.
He held his mother's hand as they walked back.

When Oliver got home, he noticed a moving truck parked near his house. The new neighbors were moving in next door! Oliver and his mom walked over to introduce themselves.

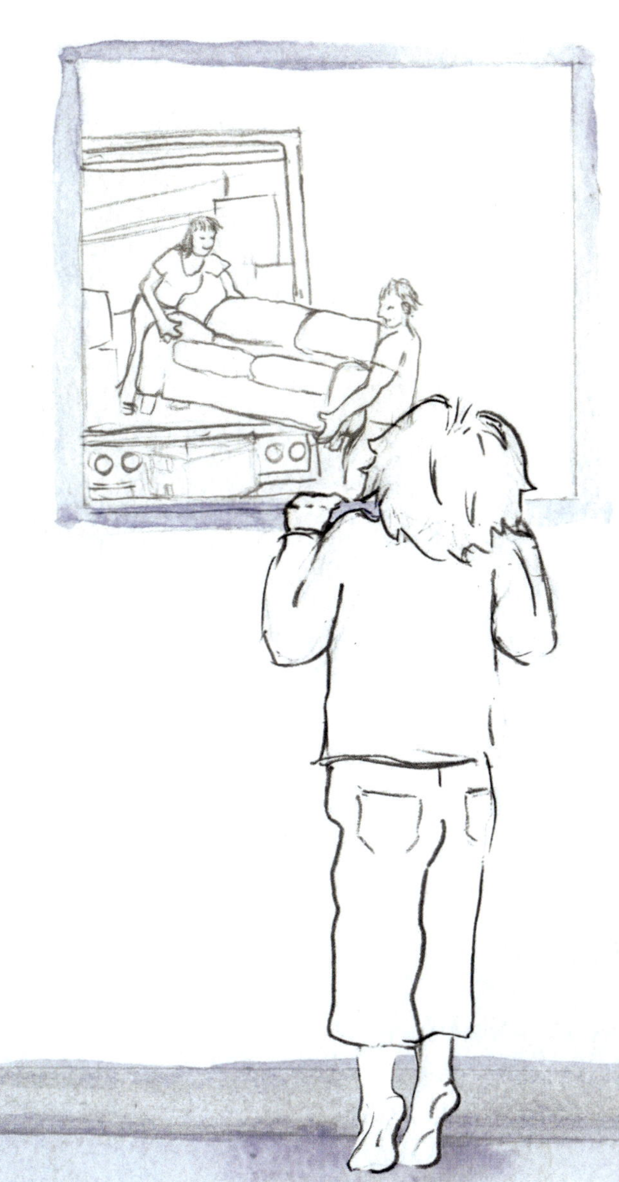

That's when Oliver met Odile.

Odile was running around with her doll. She looked so happy to be moving into a new house. She threw her doll in the air, she sang songs, she skipped, and she laughed.

Odile was very, very loud, but Oliver didn't seem to mind.

Odile joined Oliver at his house for blueberry pancakes and syrup the following morning.

They both helped Oliver's mom make the batter and mix it well. Oliver added a cup of flour, while Odile threw in the blueberries one by one as she counted them out loud.

After breakfast, Oliver showed Odile his car collection, his wooden train set, and his favorite books. Then his mom read them some stories while they had pretzels and lemonade.

Oliver and Odile had so much fun that day that they started to play together almost every day after school.

One day, Odile asked Oliver if he wanted to go to the playground with her.
Oliver wasn't very fond of the playground, but he really wanted to play with Odile, so he decided to go along.

When they got there, Oliver was happy to see that the playground was very quiet.

Oliver and Odile had fun on the slide and the swings. They laughed on the seesaw and built castles in the sandbox. Oliver was having so much fun with Odile that he didn't notice the playground had filled up with other children.

The playground was getting really noisy, but that didn't bother Oliver. When he looked around, he realized that being in crowded, noisy places wasn't always so bad after all!

A few days later, while Oliver was playing in his room, the doorbell rang. His mother answered the door and called him over. Odile was standing at the door with her mom, and when she saw Oliver, she handed him a little envelope with a card inside.

It was an invitation to Odile's birthday party.

Oliver looked at his invitation and smiled.
Then he remembered: parties are crowded and parties are loud.

But Oliver was so excited about going to Odile's party that he tried very hard not to worry about all the people who would be there or the loud music.

In fact, during the party, Oliver danced to the music. He enjoyed the noisemakers. He played all kinds of games with the other kids.

Oliver even won a prize!

And when Odile blew out the candles on her birthday cake,
Oliver was the first to clap and cheer as he cried,
"Happy birthday, Odile!"

When Oliver got home after the party, his father greeted him at the door.
"How was the party, Oliver? Did you have a good time?" he asked with his arms wide open.
Oliver ran to his dad and gave him a big hug.

"I had a great time, Dad!" he answered. "But it's nice to be back home."

One sunny day, a few weeks after Odile's party, Oliver and his mother drove by the neighborhood pool again as they were heading home. Oliver looked out the window.
His mom asked, "How about we go for a nice swim, Oliver? I think I see Odile by the pool."

The pool was pretty crowded. Oliver saw a little girl swimming with her dad. She looked a little like Odile, but Oliver didn't think it was her.

Still, the pool did look like fun, Oliver thought.

"That sounds like a great idea, Mom!" Oliver finally said with a big smile.

Even though Odile wasn't there, Oliver had a wonderful afternoon swimming, playing, and laughing with his mom and the other children at the pool.

THE END

WHAT DID YOU THINK ABOUT THE STORY?

My name is Leila. I'm a highly sensitive person, and I wrote these stories to help highly sensitive children find their own way in the world.

This story is not real, but there are lots of children like Oliver...
maybe you're a bit like him too!

Remember, in real life things can be harder to get used to or take longer to achieve than they do in story books—but that's OK!

It's always good to talk about how you feel with your family.

Here are some questions you could talk about together:

- ☆ Do you enjoy going to the playground?
- ☆ Would you like to be invited to a birthday party?
- ☆ Do you like making friends? Why is that?
- ☆ Do you have any of your own questions about the story?
- ☆ What did you like most about this story?

Leila Boukarim was born in Lebanon, raised in several countries, and now resides in Singapore with her husband and two wonderful children. Since discovering her eldest was a highly sensitive child, Leila has dedicated herself to shedding light on what it's like to have a child who doesn't like the playground, sprinklers, or parties, and to writing books that speak to these extraordinary children. This is her first children's book.

Barbara Moxham was born in Munich, raised in Sydney and currently calls Singapore home. She is the mother of two excitable, loving young boys who are like chalk and cheese: one being sensitive and sweet and the other hilarious and hyper. Travel has given her kids incredible experiences and helped them face their fears. Barbara is so excited to be able to illustrate books for children who feel the world in such an intense way.

Made in the USA
Coppell, TX
18 June 2021